Rockwood and Limehouse Ontario in Colour Photos, Saving Our History One Photo at a Time

Photography
by Barbara Raué
2014

Series Name:
Cruising Ontario

Book 83 - Rockwood

Cover photo: 130 Guelph Street, Rockwood

Series Name: Cruising Ontario
Saving Our History One Photo at a Time

Other Books by Barbara Raue

Coins of Gold

Arrows, Indians and Love

The Life and Times of Barbara
Volume 1: Inventions That Have Enhanced My Life
Volume 2: Entertainment That I Have Enjoyed
Volume 3: East Coast Trips
Volume 4: Olympics Have Always Intrigued Me
Volume 5: Wonders of the World
Volume 6: Caribbean Cruises We Have Enjoyed
Volume 7: Animals
Volume 8: Storms and Other Major Disasters in My Lifetime
Volume 9: Wars, Terrorist Attacks and Major Disasters

The Cromwell Family Book

Laura Secord Discovered

Visit Barbara's website to view all of her books
http://barbararaue.ca

Rockwood

Rockwood is located on Highway 7 between Acton and the city of Guelph. The Eramosa River runs through the centre of the village.

Early settlers to this area were Quakers. John Harris, the first settler, erected a shanty in 1821. In 1840 Colonel Henry Strange settled and brought further development to the area which became known as Strange's Mills. Strange was the Deputy Provincial Surveyor and he opened a lime quarry which provided stone for building mills. In the 1850s the community became known as Rockwood which reflected the lovely river valley, mixed forest, high rocky hills, and geological potholes. The Eramosa River provided power for John Gamble's sawmill which was the first in Wellington County. Grist, flour, oatmeal, stave, and woollen mills followed. A post office was opened in 1853 and the Grand Trunk Railway opened a station in 1855.

Limehouse

Limehouse is a community in the Town of Halton Hills in southern Ontario. It has a population of about 800 people and its closest neighbours are Georgetown and Acton. Limehouse has many hills, trails and a small school.

Table of Contents

Rockwood

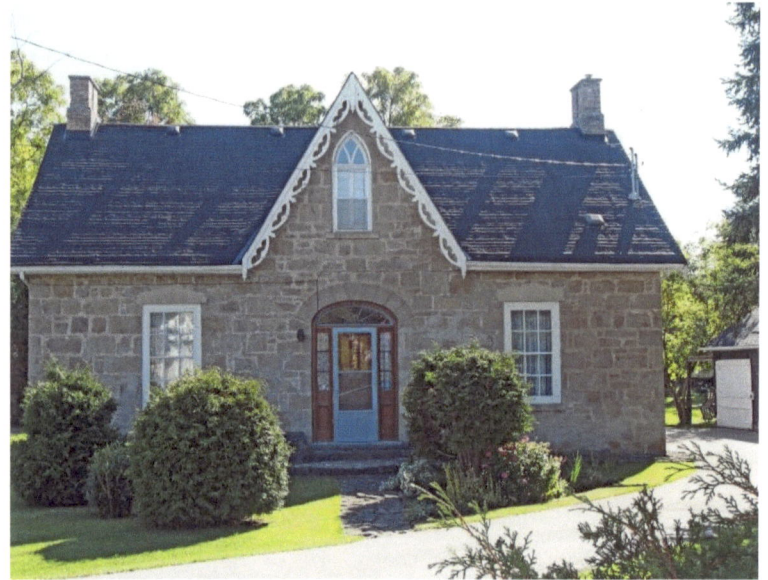

Main Street – Gothic Revival, verge board trim on gable, sidelight, transom window, arched voussoirs

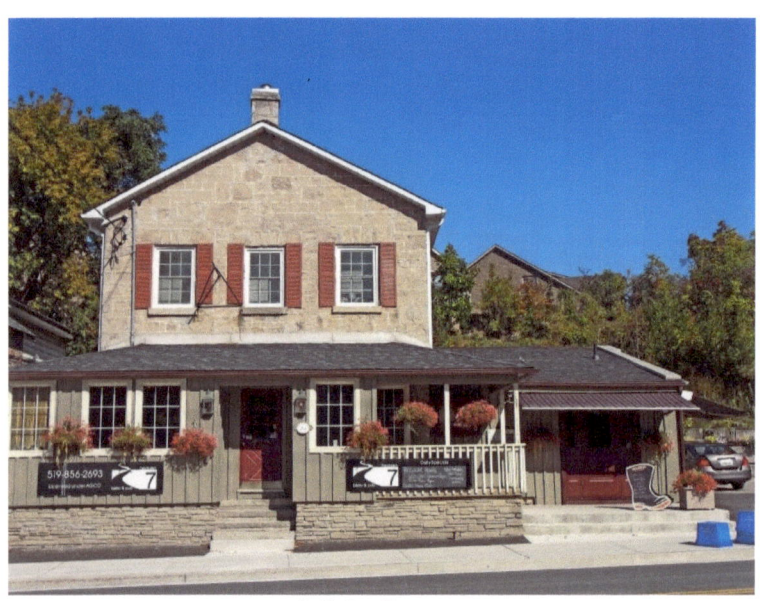

Main Street

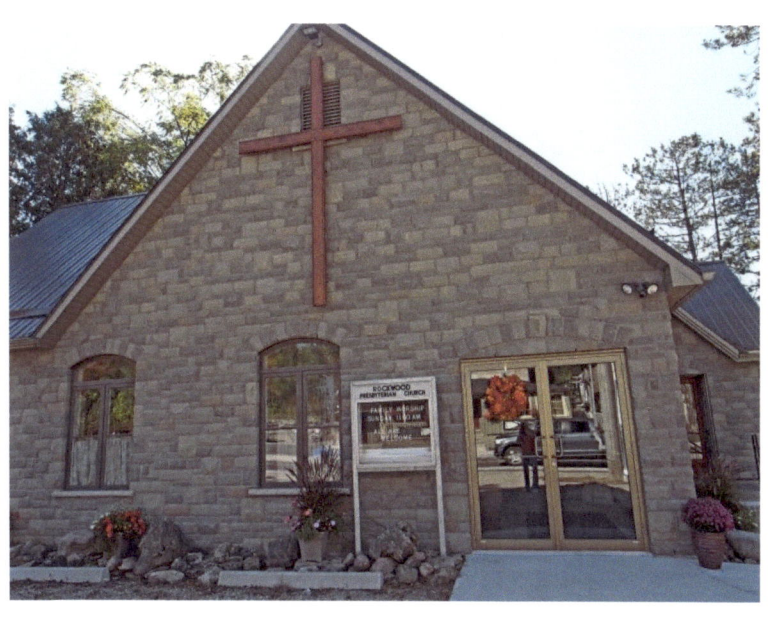

Main Street - Rockwood Presbyterian Church

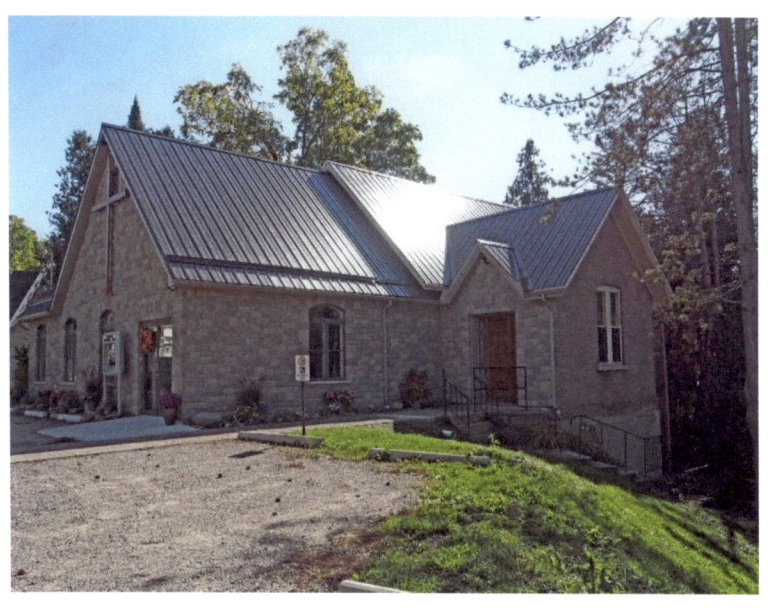

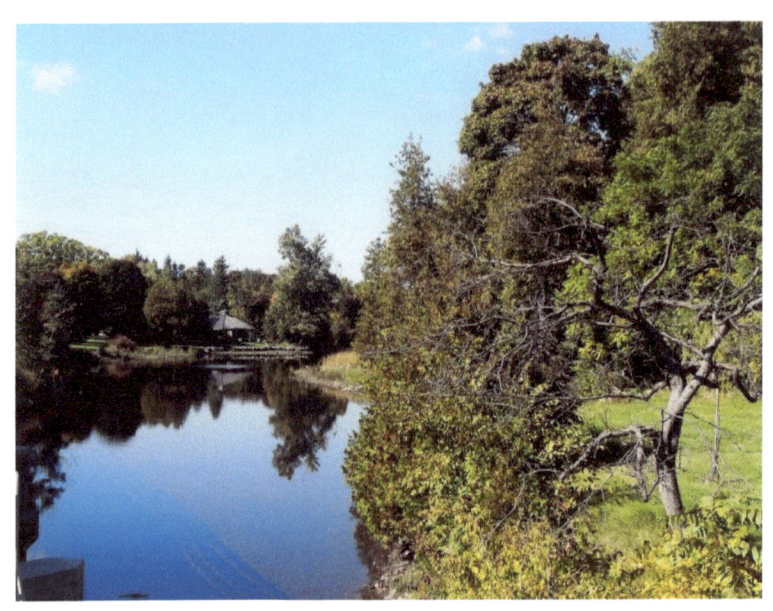

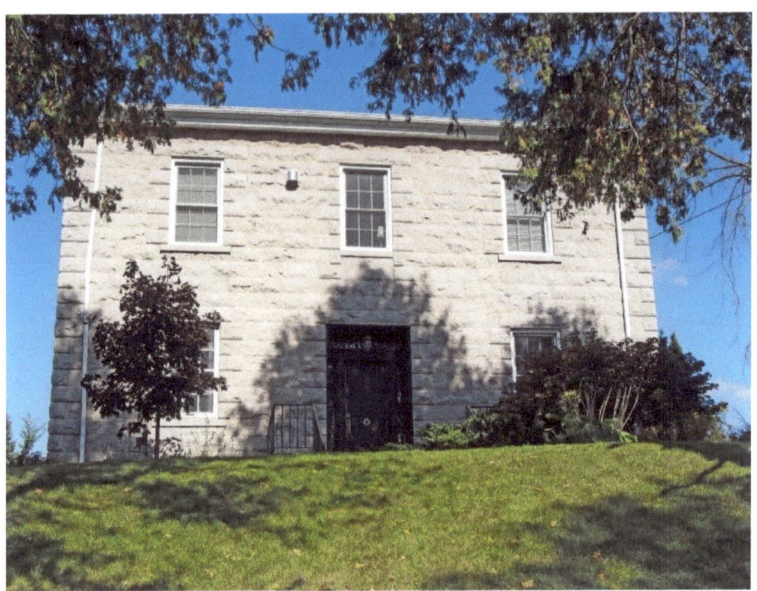

Limestone house

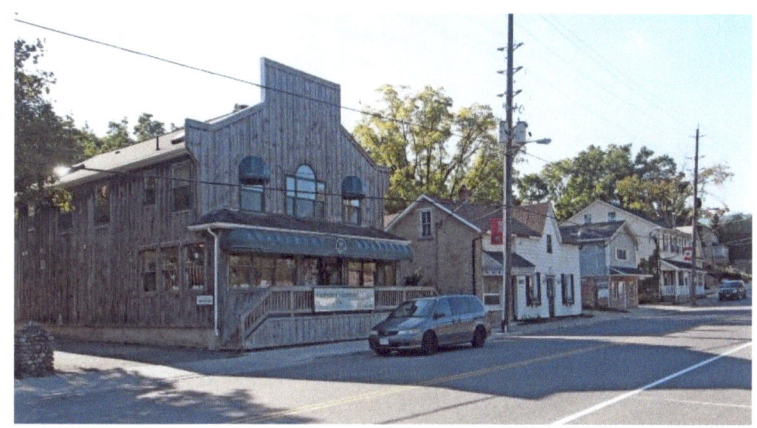

Main Street

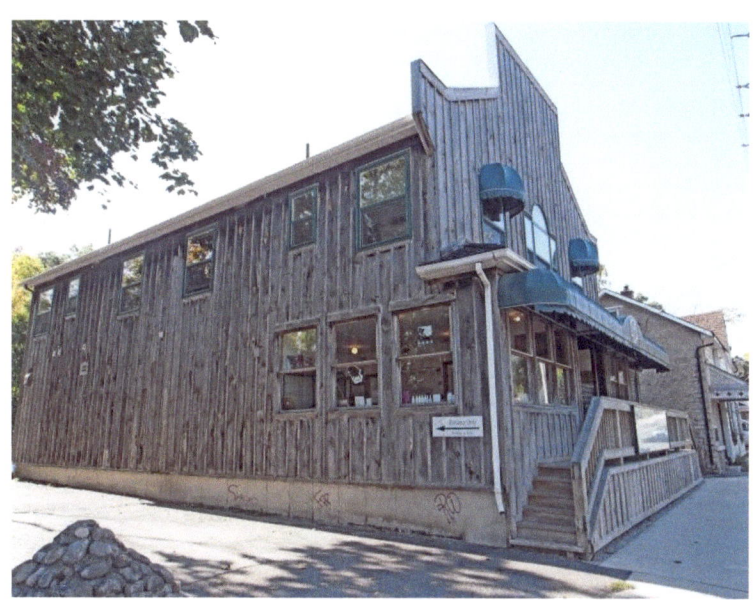

Main Street - Rockwood Veterinary Clinic – wood building

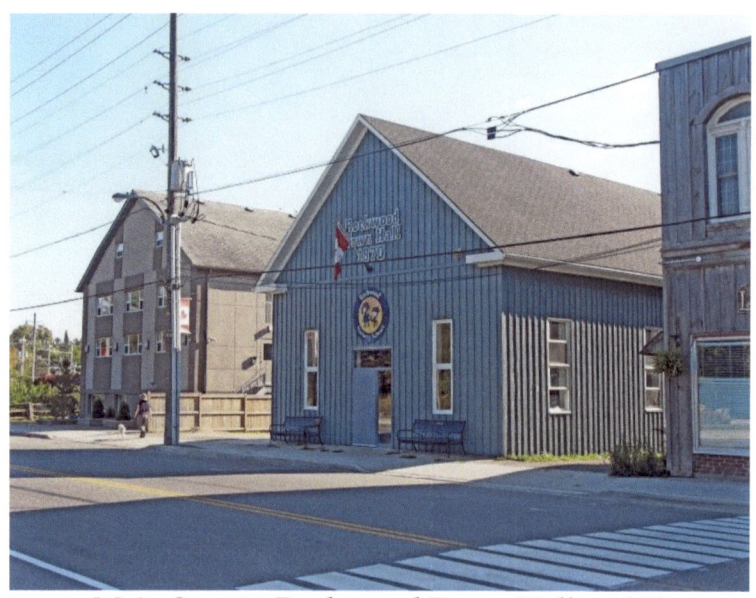

Main Street - Rockwood Town Hall – 1870

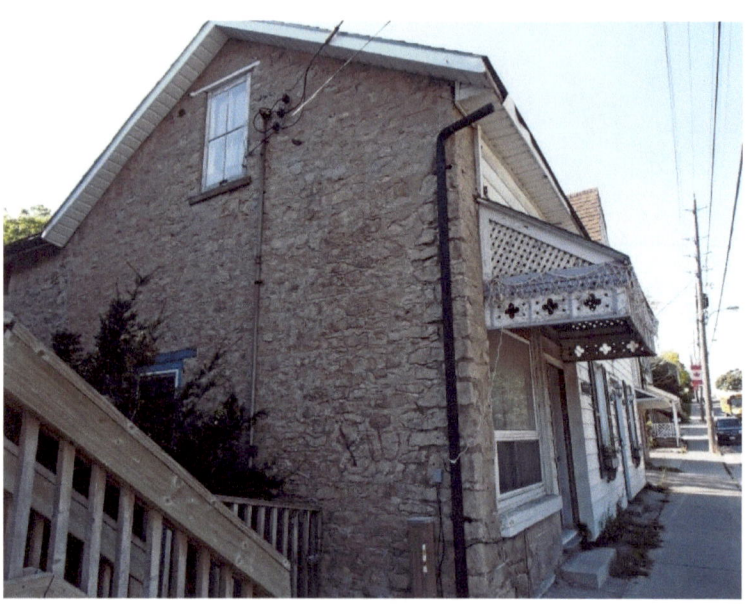

Limestone building

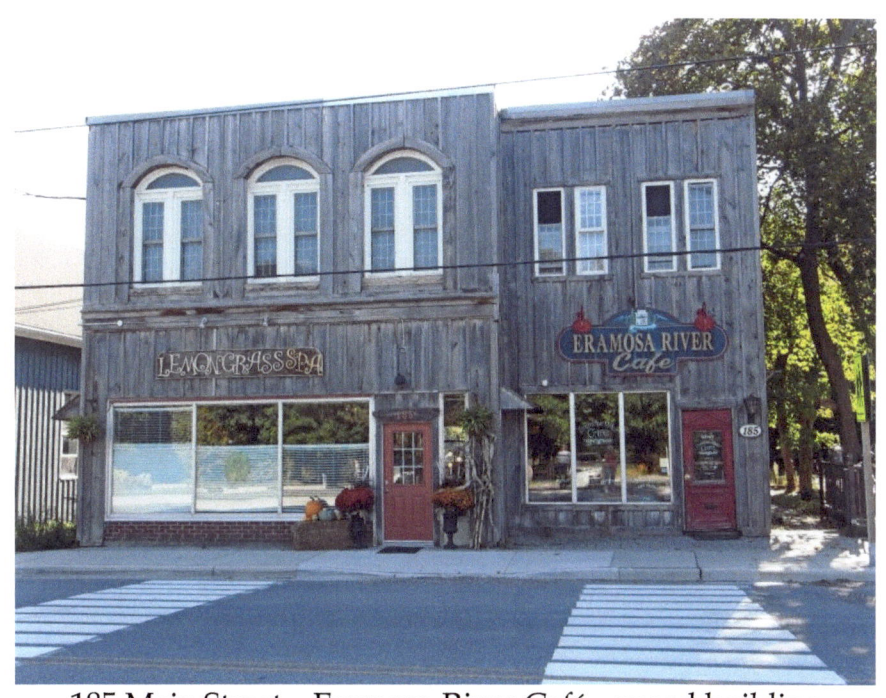

185 Main Street – Eramosa River Café – wood building

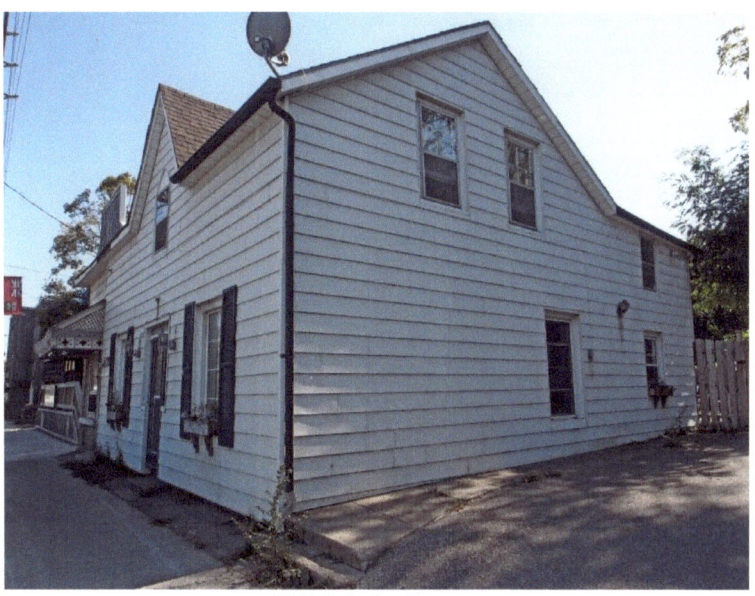

173 Main Street

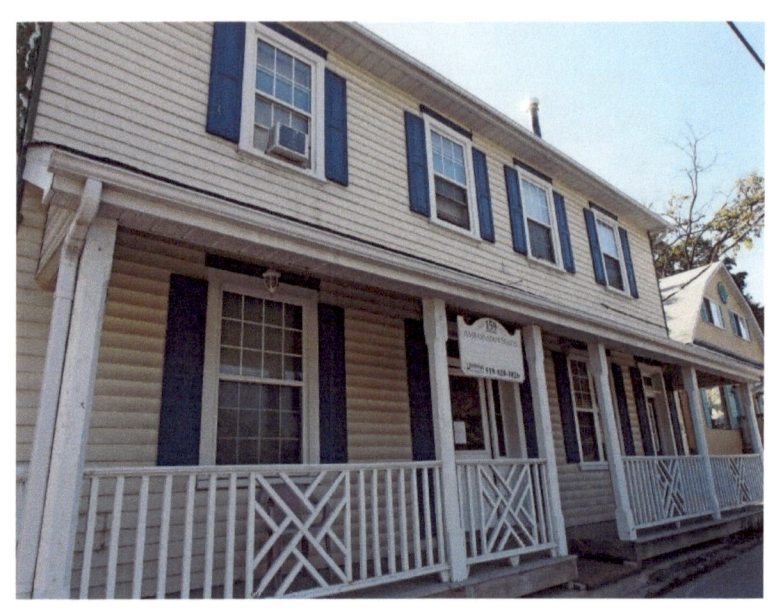

159 Main Street – Ambassador Suites

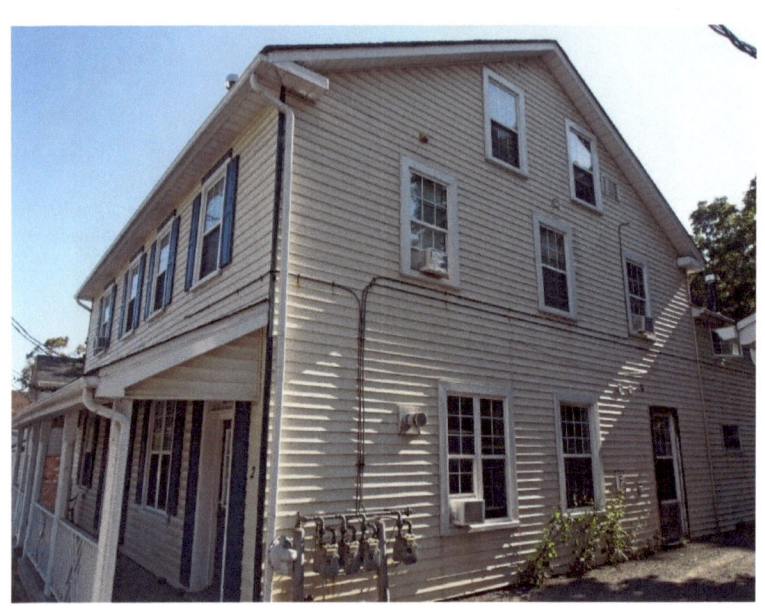

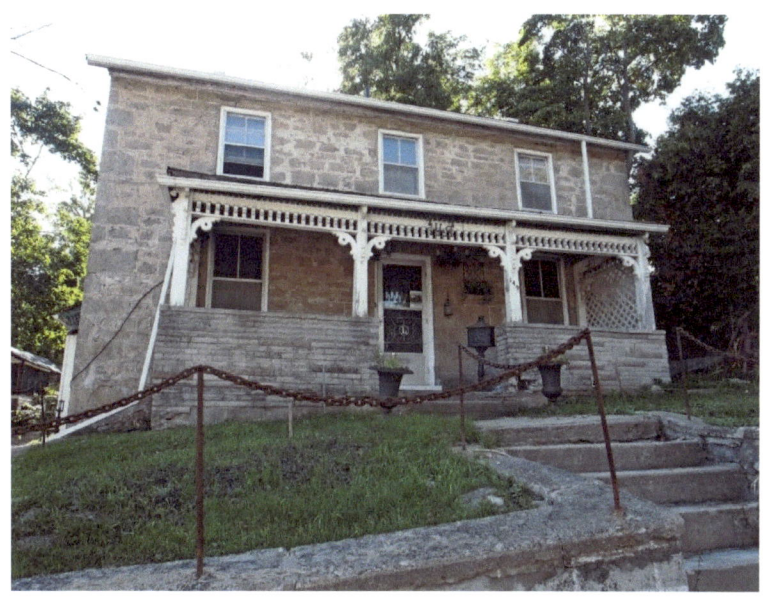

149 Main Street – limestone house, cobblestone architecture

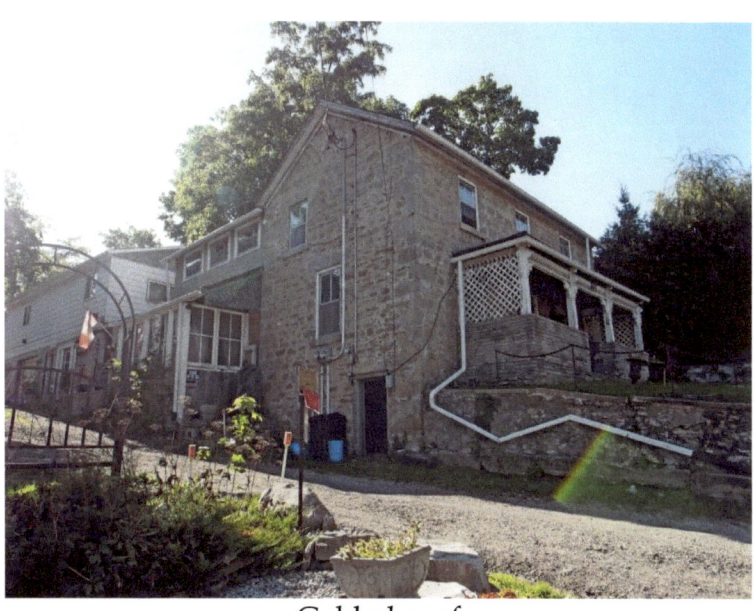

Gabled roof

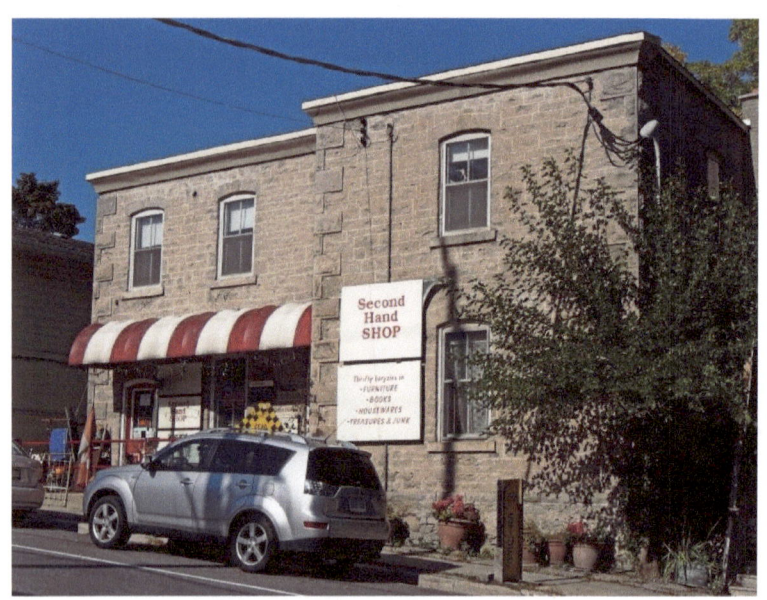

Main Street – corner quoins

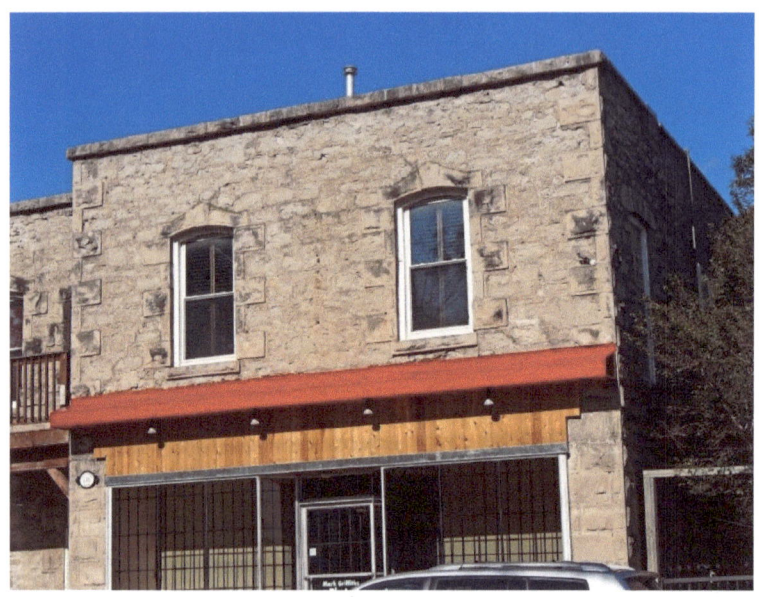

Main Street – limestone building

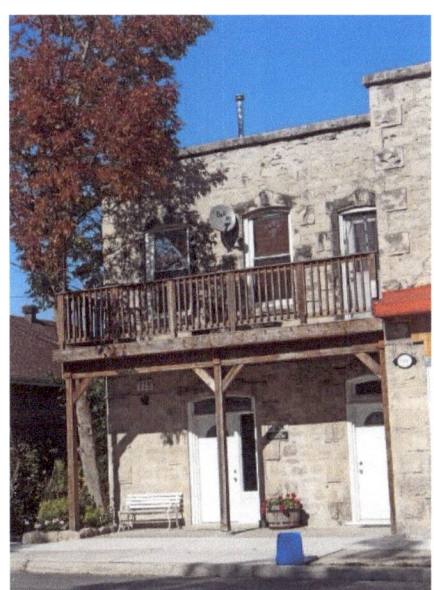

118 Main Street

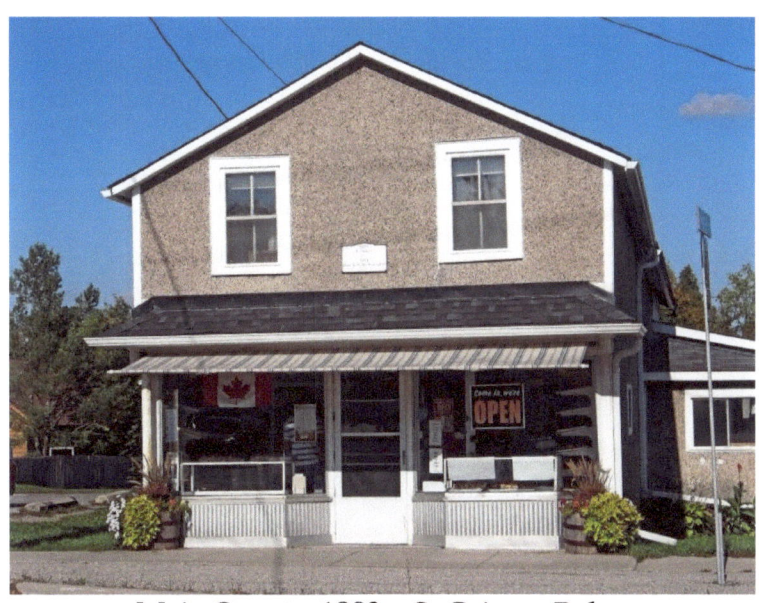

Main Street - 1893 – S. Grieve, Baker
1914 – Pete and Nellie Saunders, Baker

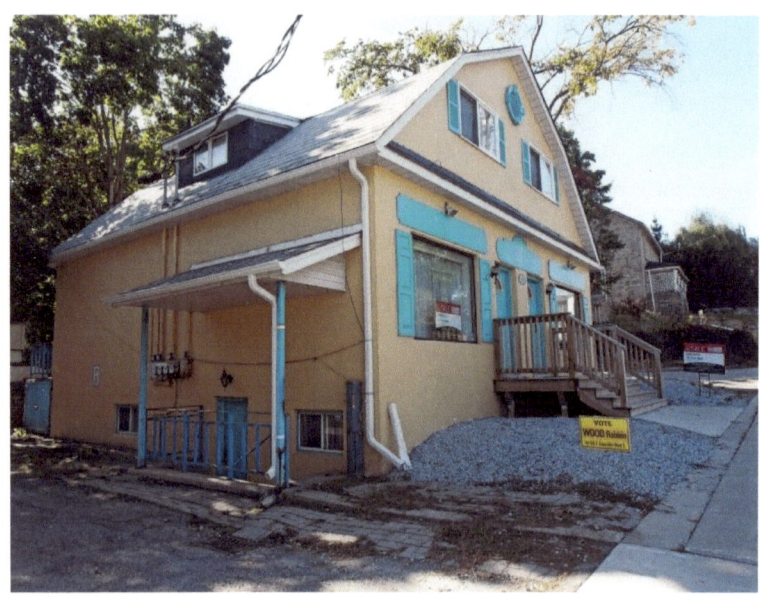

155 Main Street

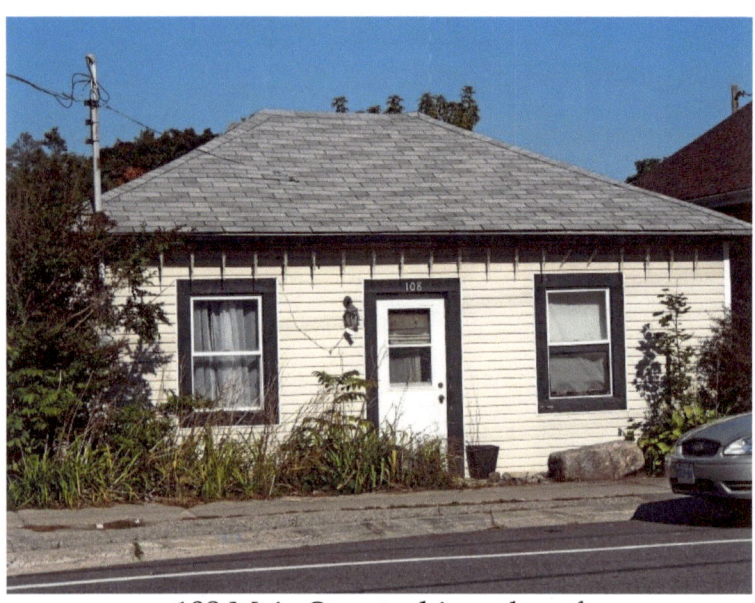

108 Main Street – hipped roof

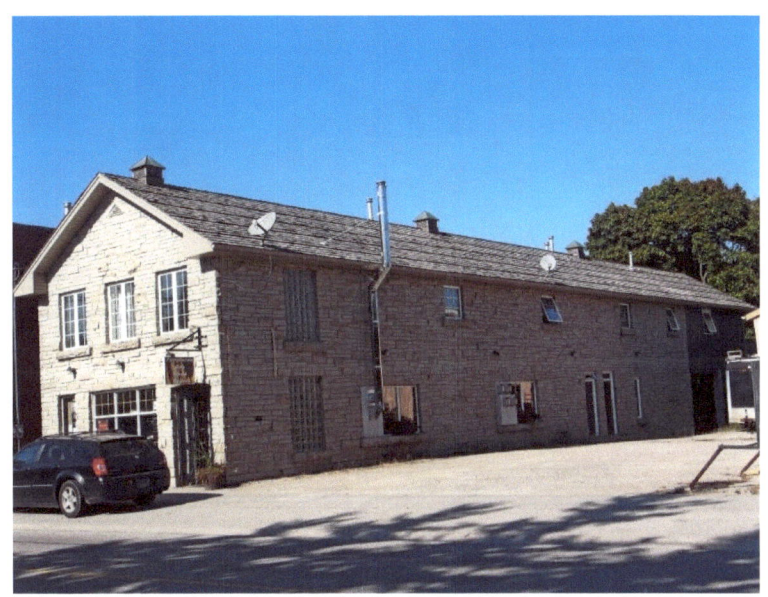

138 Main Street

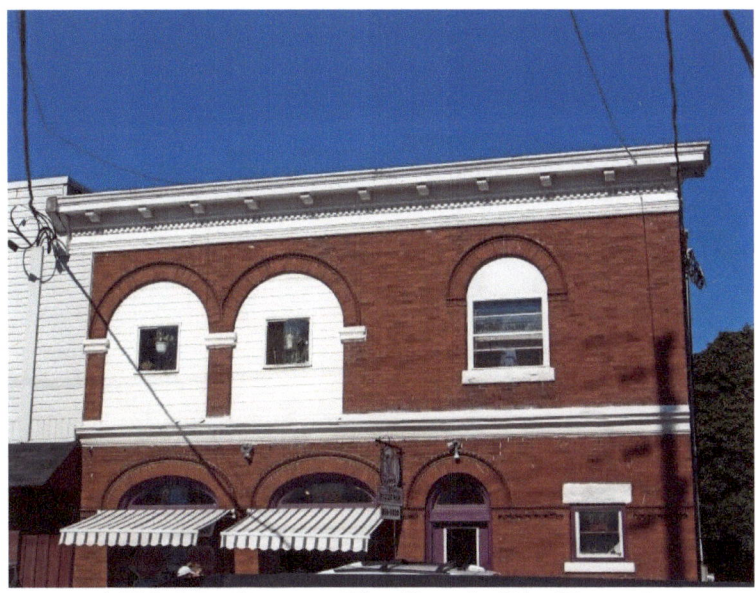

142 Main Street – The Purple Pig Pizzeria
Dentil moulding, Romanesque style window arches

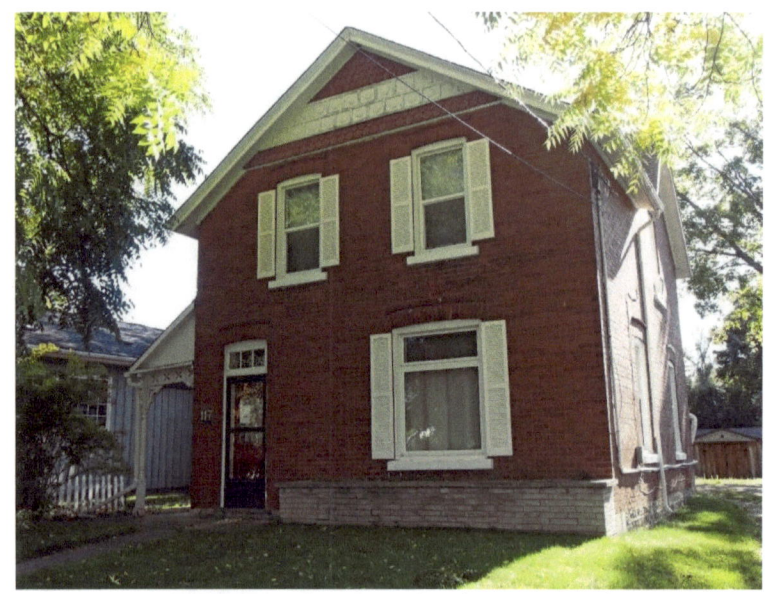

117 Main Street – Gothic Revival

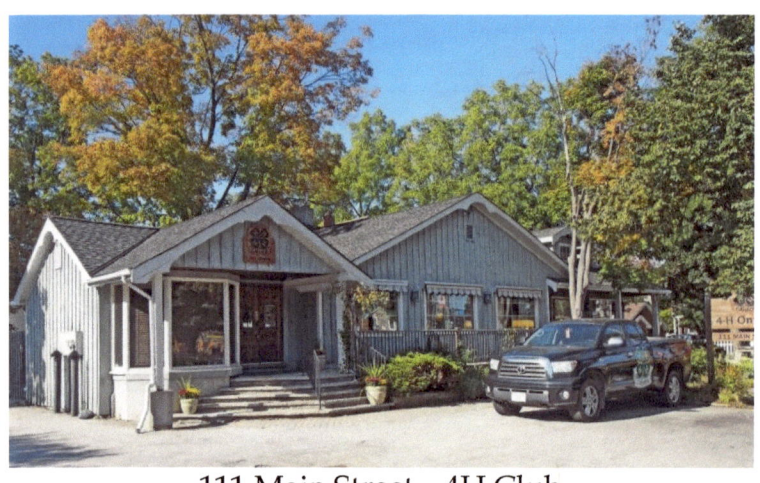

111 Main Street – 4H Club

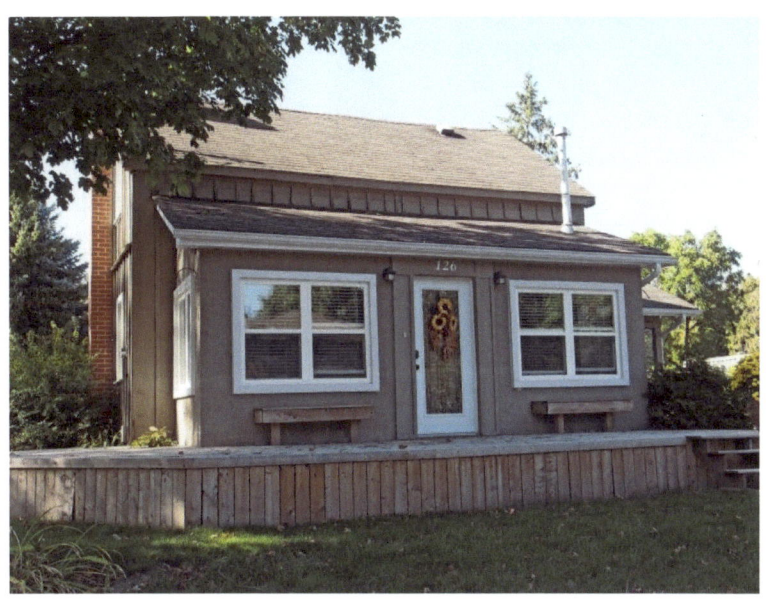

126 Main Street – board and batten

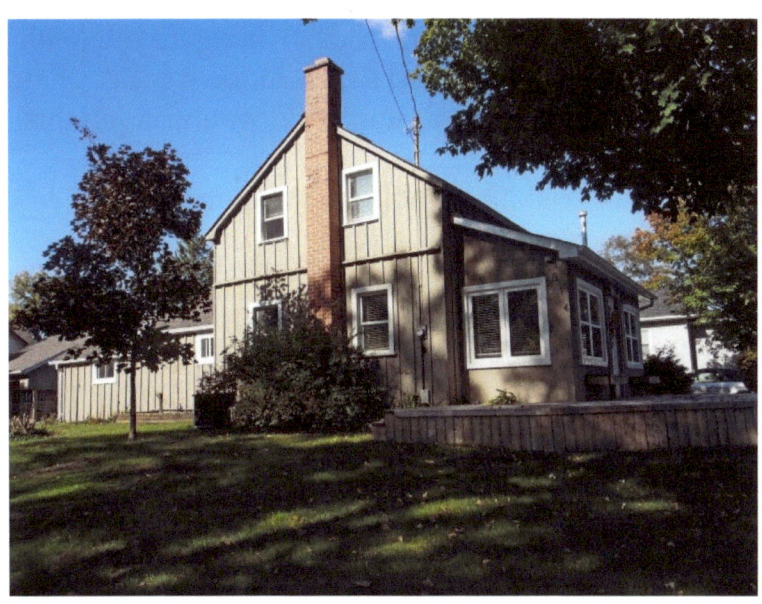

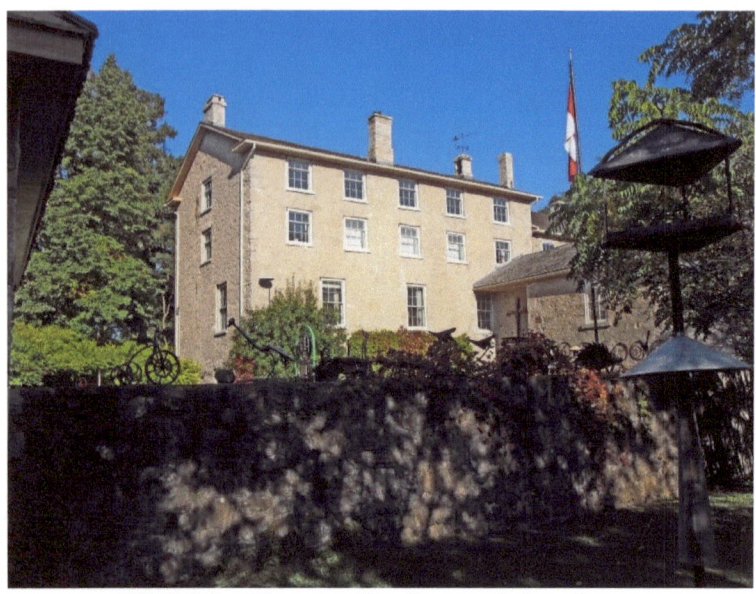

477 Main Street – Rockwood Academy

Georgian style - three-storey stone building with limestone walls, rough-cut quoins, symmetrical five-bay façade with double-hung six-over-six wood sash windows with a central door with a portico and a transom window and sidelights.

Low-pitched cedar-shingle gable roof with many small brick and stone chimneys

The owner's bedrooms still exist on the second floor, as do the students' bedrooms on the third floor. The south wing still contains the classroom below the student bedrooms. The west wing remains unaltered and contains a carriage house on the ground floor with a gymnasium above.

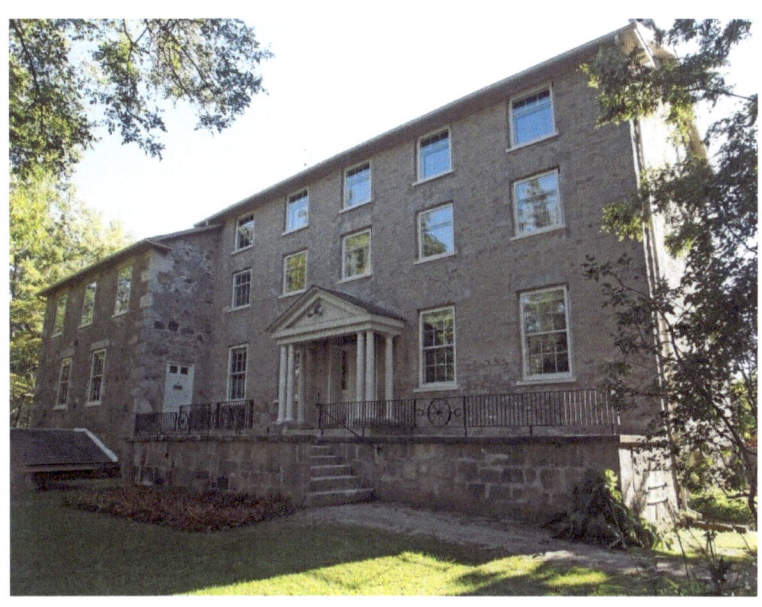

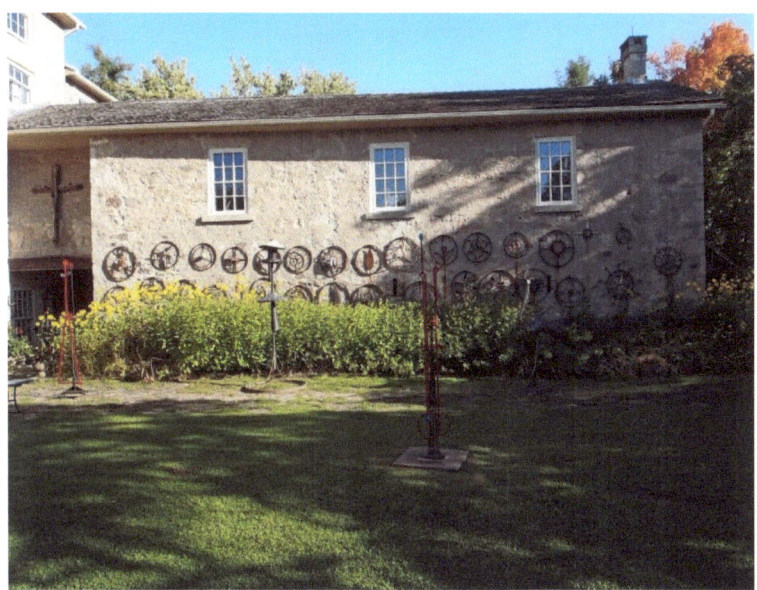

Covered carriage-way between the main building and the carriage house (to the left of the picture)

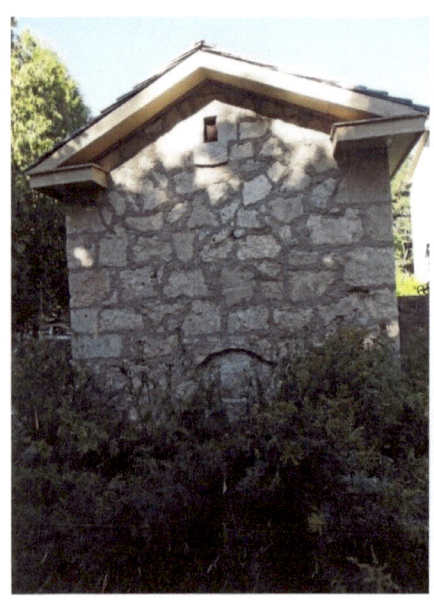
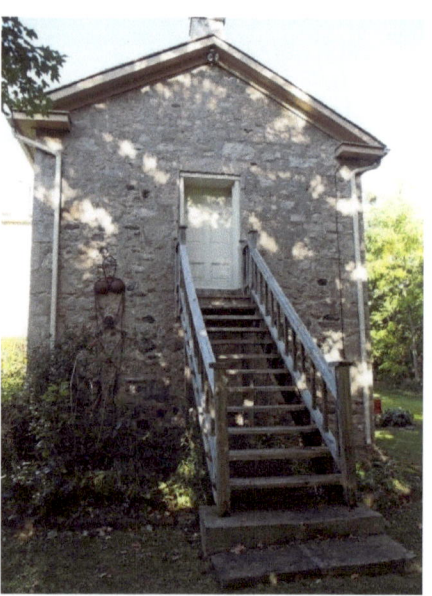

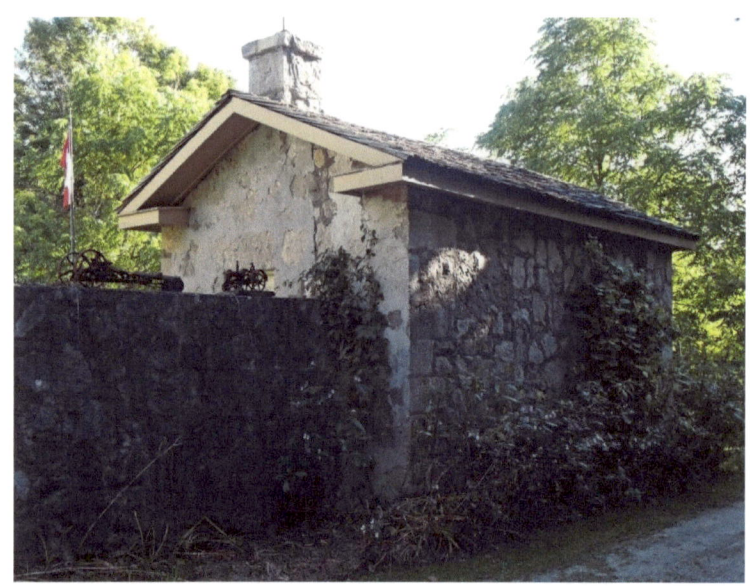

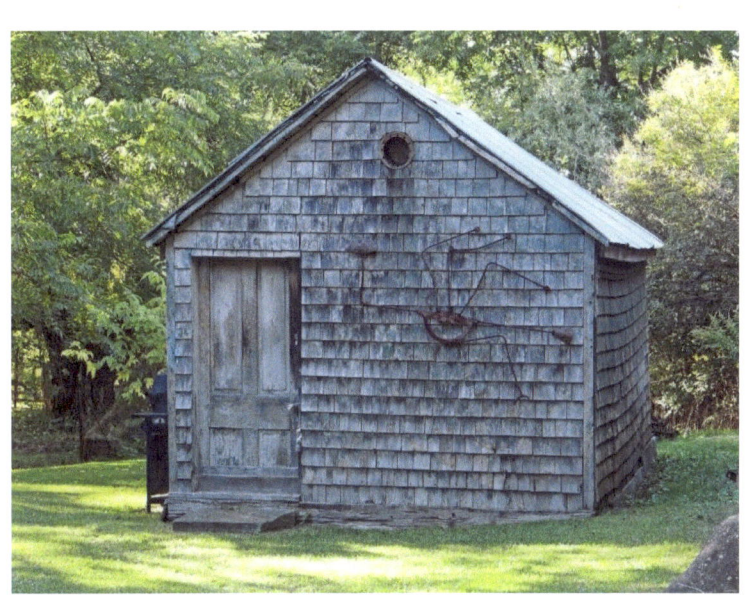

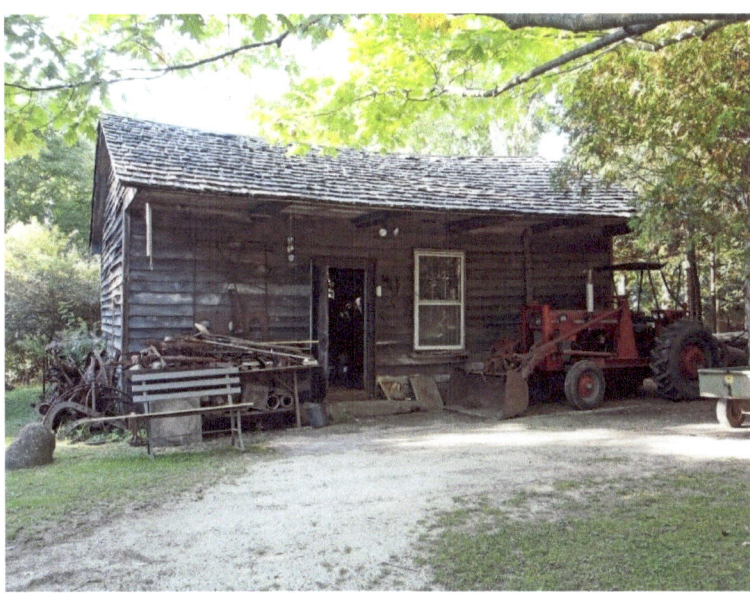

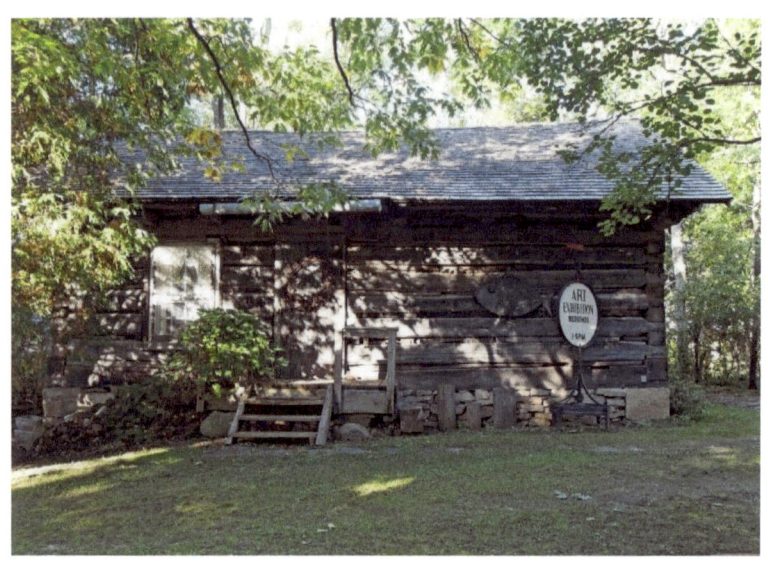

Rockwood Academy

A pioneer boarding school for boys was opened in 1850 by William Wetherald, an English Quaker from Yorkshire who had emigrated to Canada in 1835. The original log building was replaced by the present stone structure in 1853. The Academy became known for its high academic standards; this was at the time when the public school system was still developing in Upper Canada. In 1864 Donald McCaig and Alexander McMillan purchased the school and added two wings to accommodate a storeroom, a gymnasium, a large classroom, and extra dormitories. They introduced commercial courses. The school remained in operation until 1882 when the Ontario Public School system became accepted.

Among its former pupils were Honourable A. S. Hardy, fourth premier of Ontario; Sir Adam Beck, founder of the province's hydro-electric system; and James J. Hill, pioneer railway magnate.

After the academy closed, the building remained and was used as a woolen mill for a few years before remaining vacant until 1900 when the Gordon family bought it to use as a farmhouse. It had fallen into disrepair by 1960 when Josef Drenters purchased it. He spent many years working on the restoration of the old stone building as well as a log barn and chapel on the property, as well as continuing his career as a sculptor.

Born in 1930 in The Netherlands, Josef's youth was spent in classical studies preparing for the priesthood. At the age of 14 he began to take drawing instructions from a local artist, Willem van Ejendhoven. Yosef was also influenced by his father, a skilled blacksmith, who was adept at making small works in forged iron.

In 1951 after giving up his monastic life, he came to Canada with his family and first settled in British Columbia. His first years in Canada were spent working as a lumberjack, a rancher, a miner and a farmer. In 1954 the family moved to Ontario and purchased a large farm on Highway 24 north of Guelph, where in 1958 Yosef began experimenting in sculpture after several years of painting.

His first solo exhibition was at the Ontario Agricultural College. In 1960 his work was exhibited in Toronto and he was heralded as a major Canadian sculptor.

The Canadian Department of Trade and Commerce commissioned him to create a sculpture for the Tokyo Trade Fair in 1965. His *Pioneer Family* won the competition for sculpture for the Ontario Pavilion at Expo 67, and he was commissioned to create a giant toy horse for La Ronde, an amusement park in Montreal, Quebec.

Drenters bequeathed the property to the Ontario Heritage Foundation under the condition that his family would still be able to live in it. His sudden death in the winter of 1983 brought to an early close the distinguished career of a major Canadian sculptor, artist and preservationist.

His son Andreas continues to live in the house and makes metal works from scrap iron.

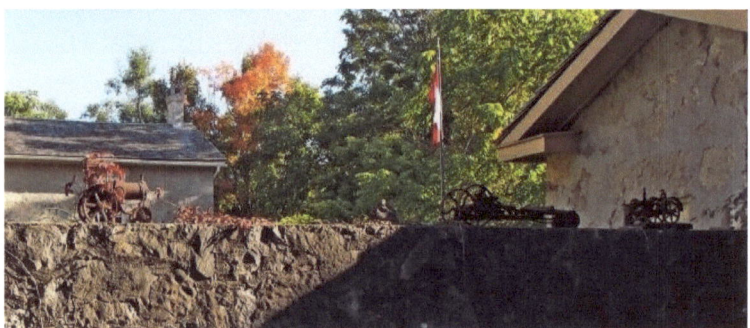

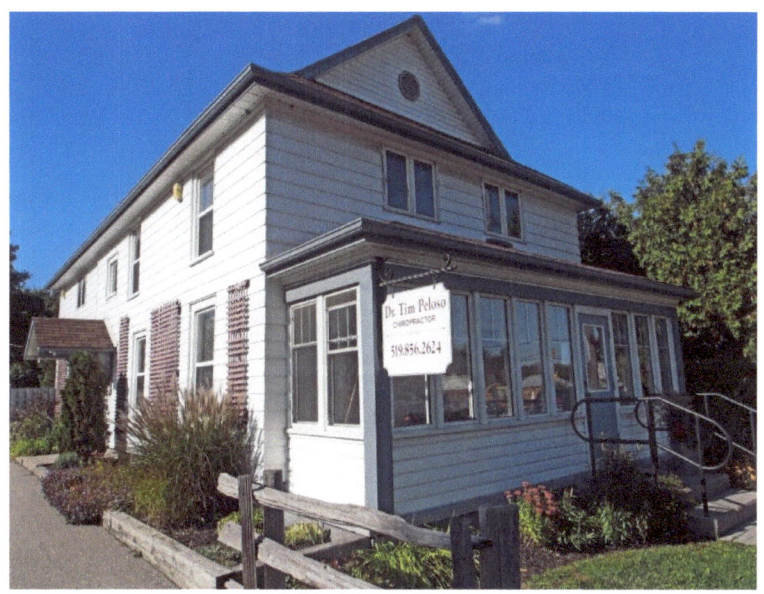

118 Alma Street

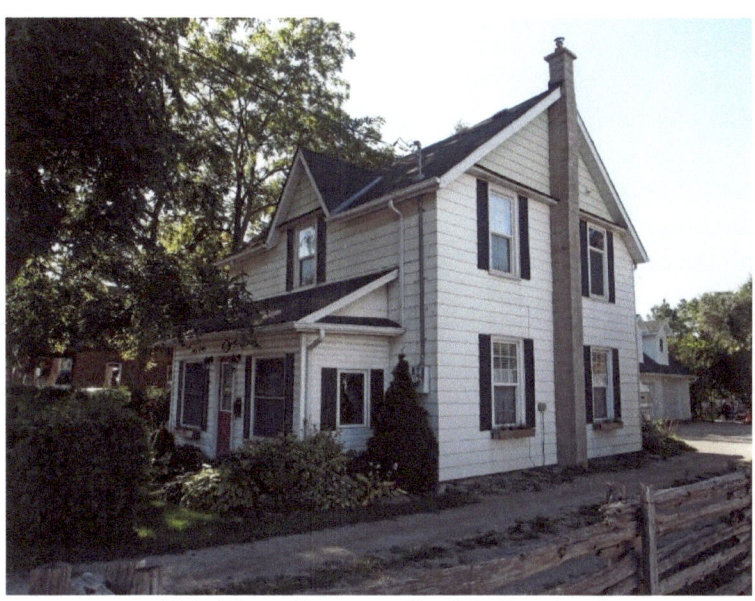

124 Alma Street – Gothic Revival

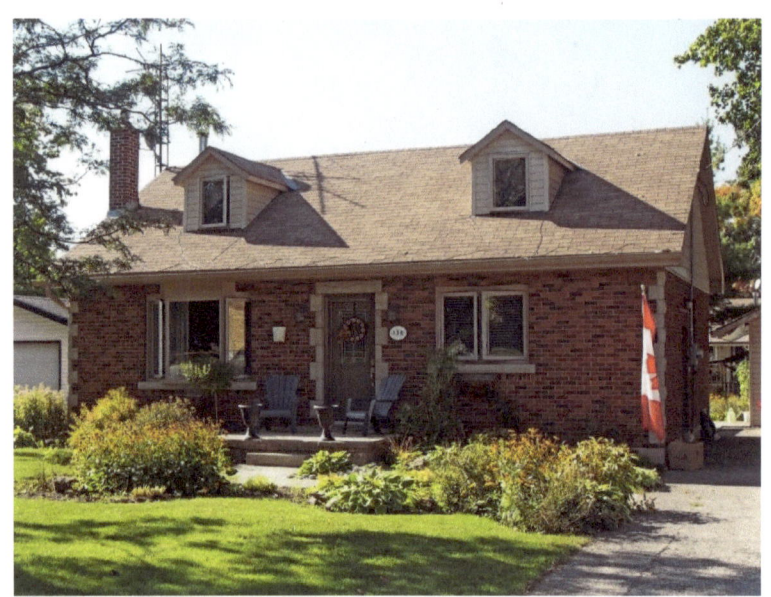

138 Alma Street – dormers in attic

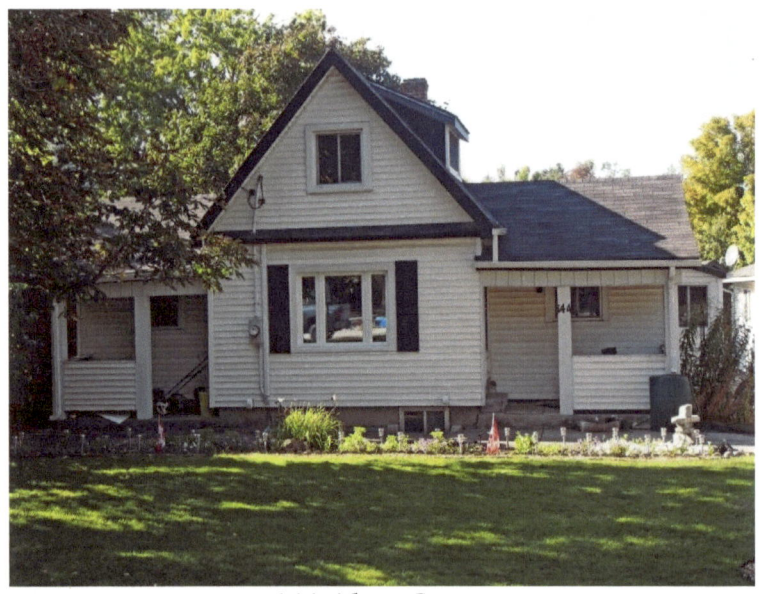

144 Alma Street

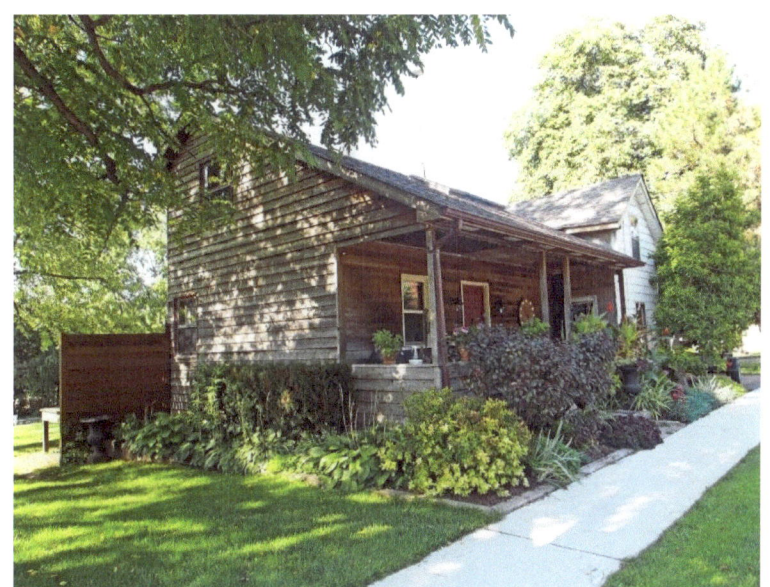

150 Alma Street

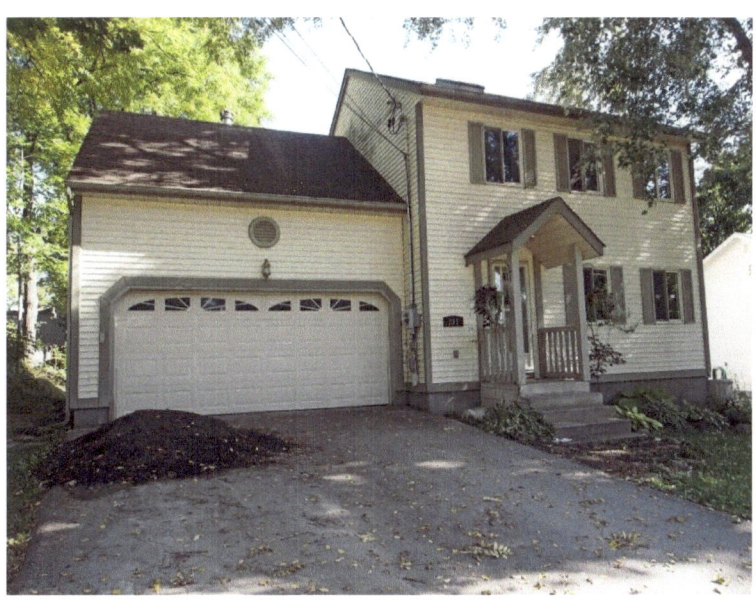

211 Guelph Street

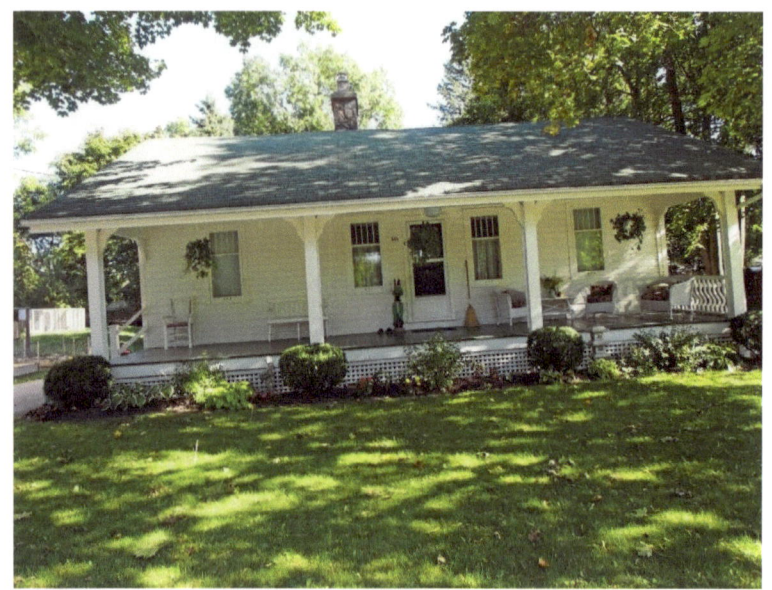

213 Guelph Street

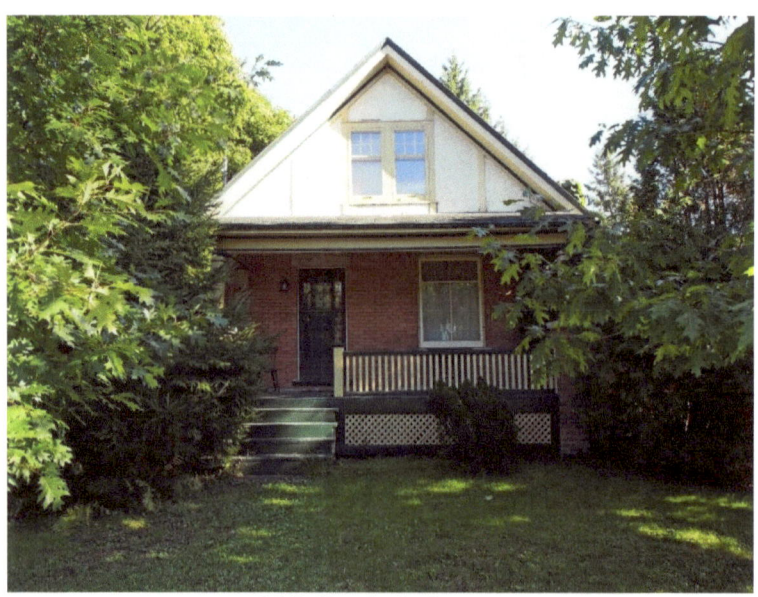

225 Guelph Street

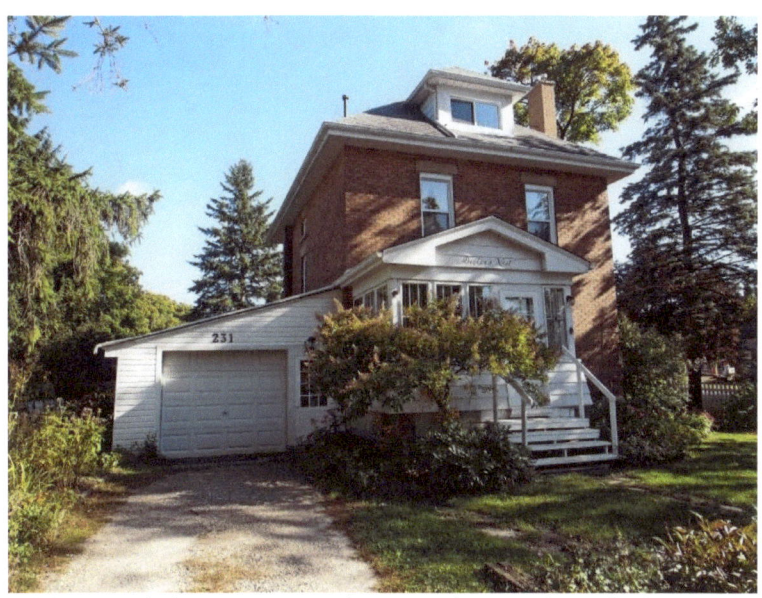

231 Guelph Street – Italianate, hipped roof, dormer

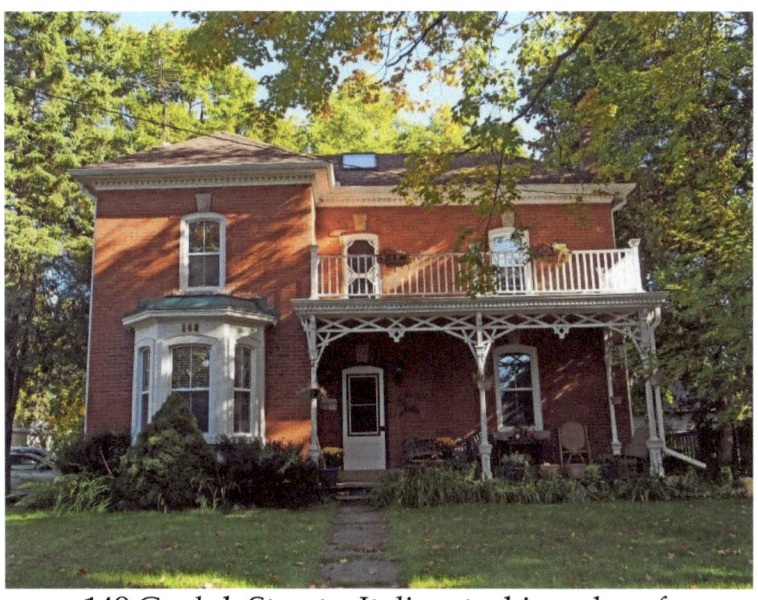

149 Guelph Street – Italianate, hipped roof,
balcony on second floor, bay window

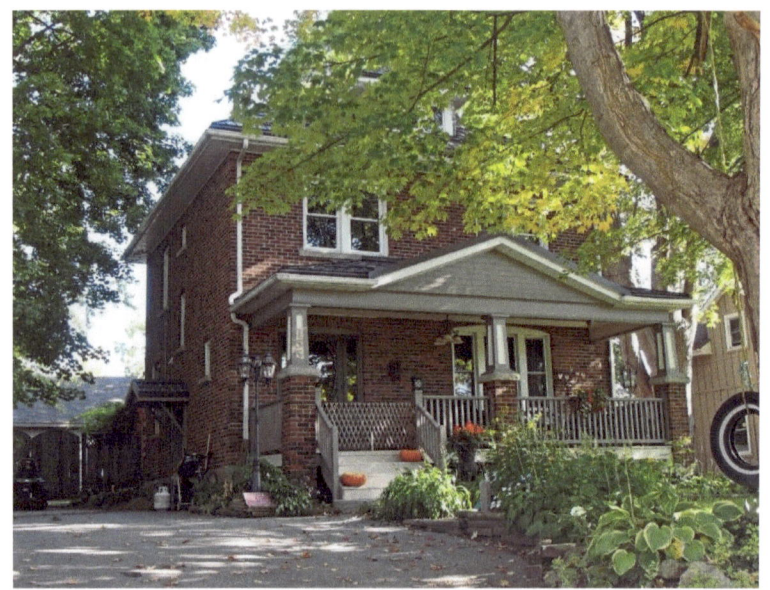

155 Guelph Street

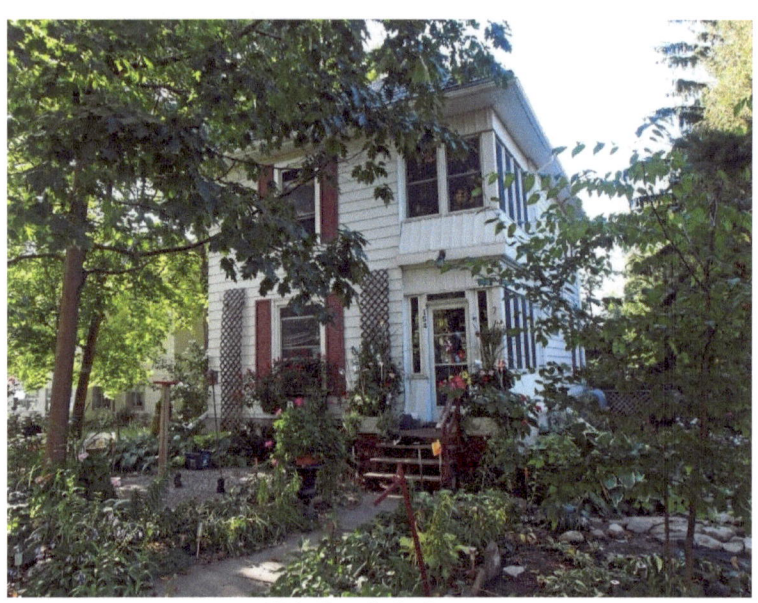

154 Guelph Street

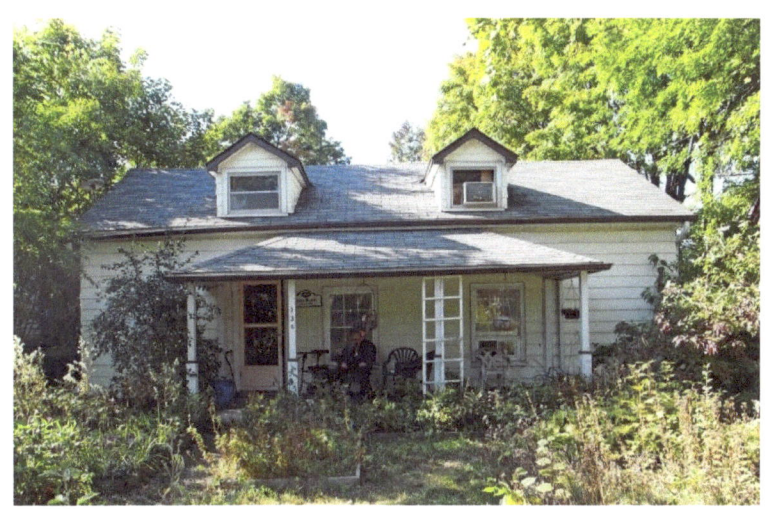

136 Guelph Street – the oldest home in the town,
built in 1823 by early settler John Harris

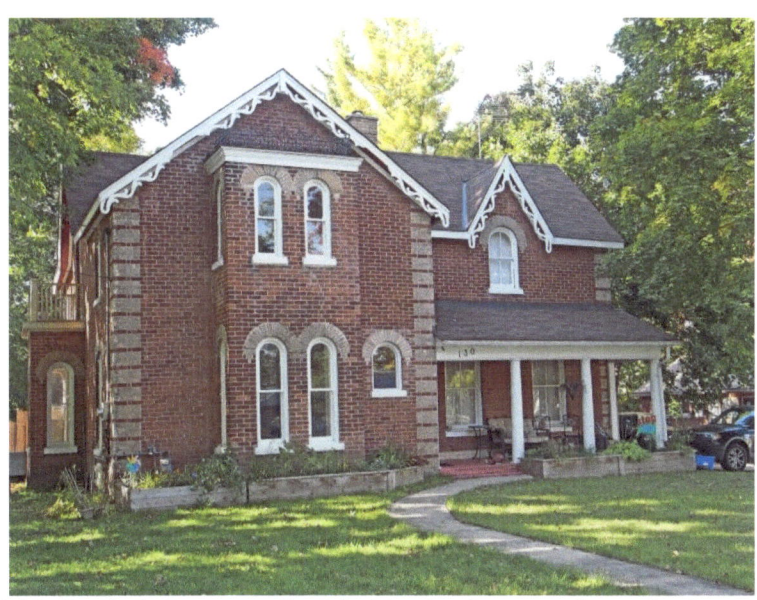

130 Guelph Street – Gothic Revival, verge board trim on
gables, corner quoins, arched voussoirs,
two-storey tower-like bay

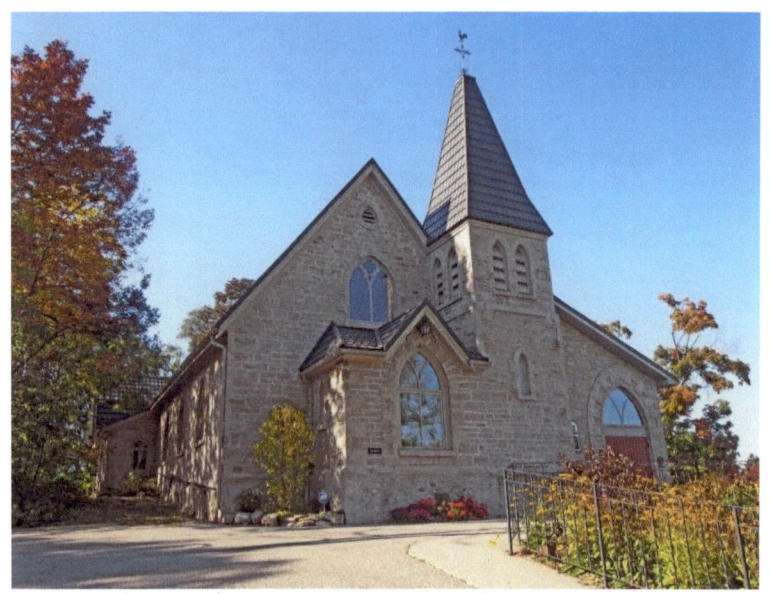

112 Guelph Street - St. John's Anglican Church – 1881
- limestone

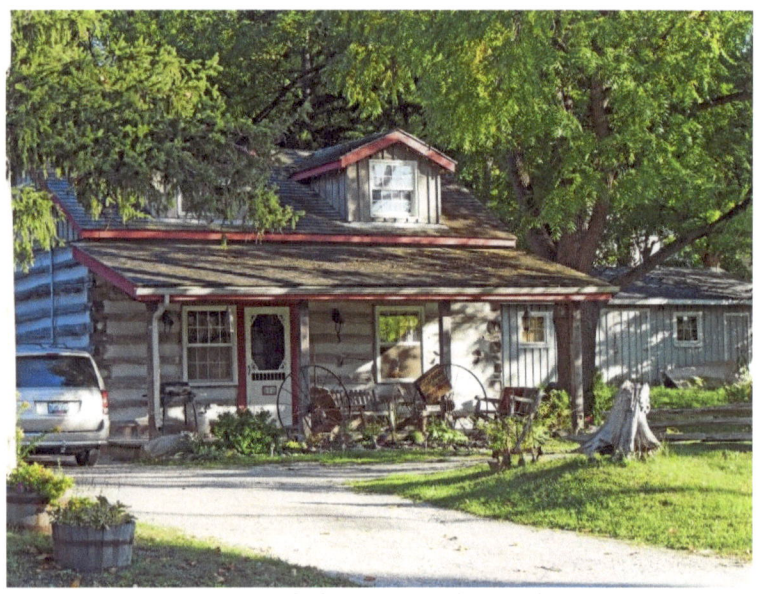

145 Guelph Street – log cabin

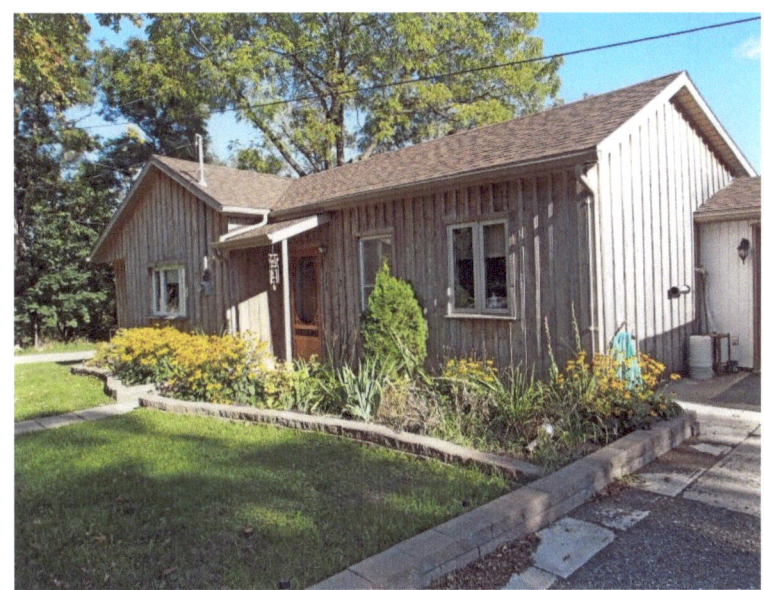

Balaclava Street – board and batten

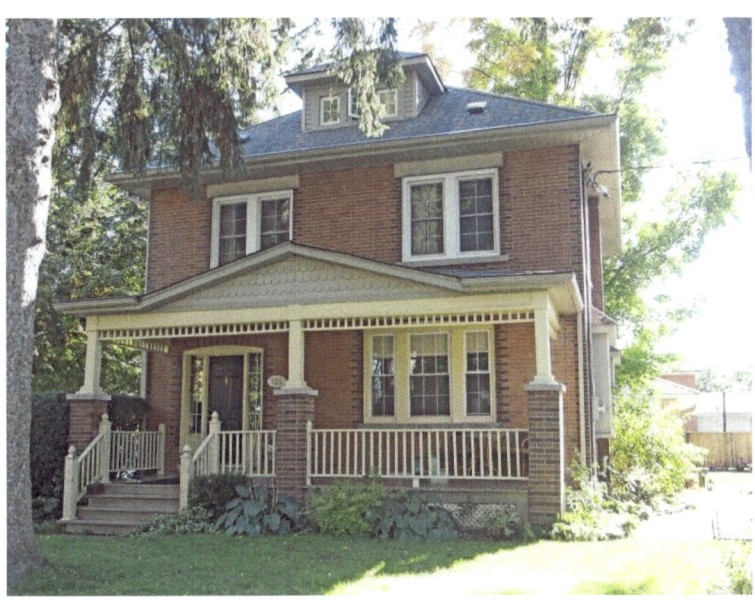

125 Richardson Street – Italianate, hipped roof, dormer in attic

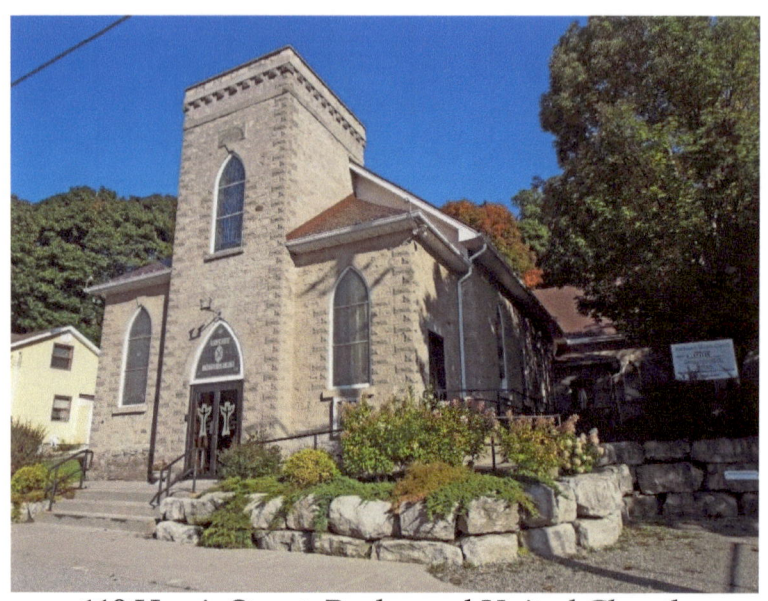

119 Harris Street, Rockwood United Church

Limehouse

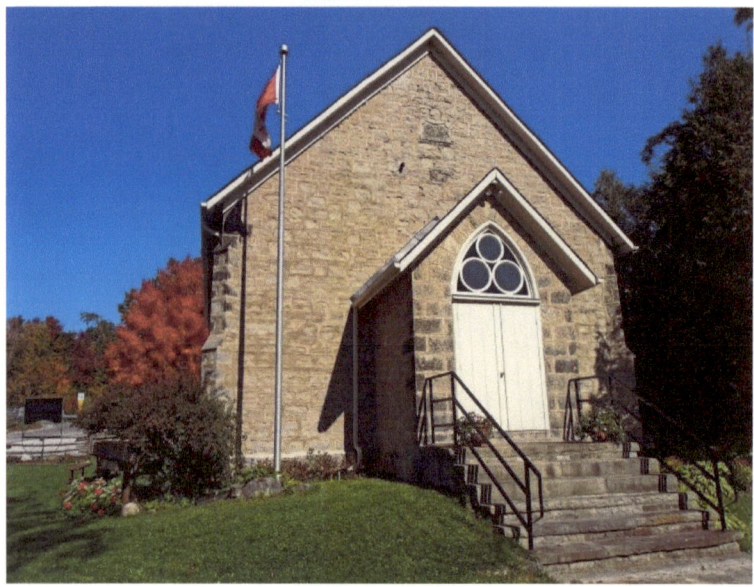

Limehouse Memorial Hall – former Horeb Methodist
Episcopal Church – 1877

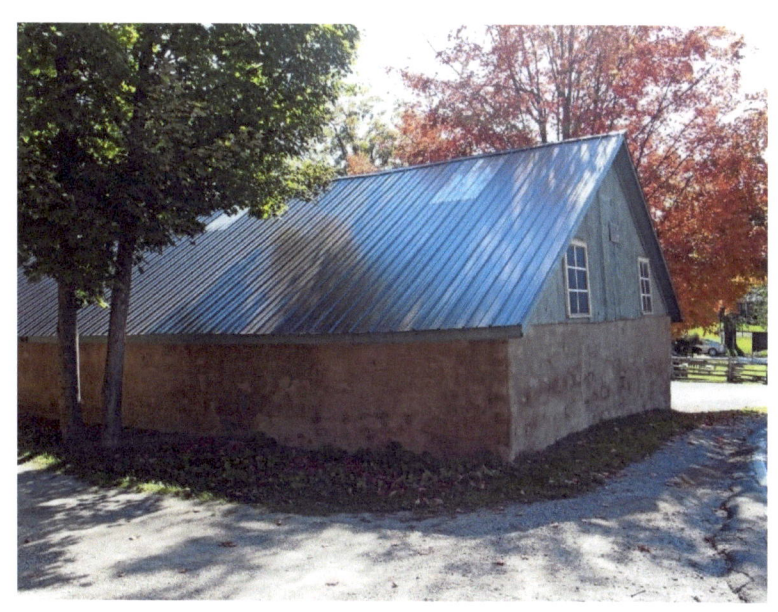

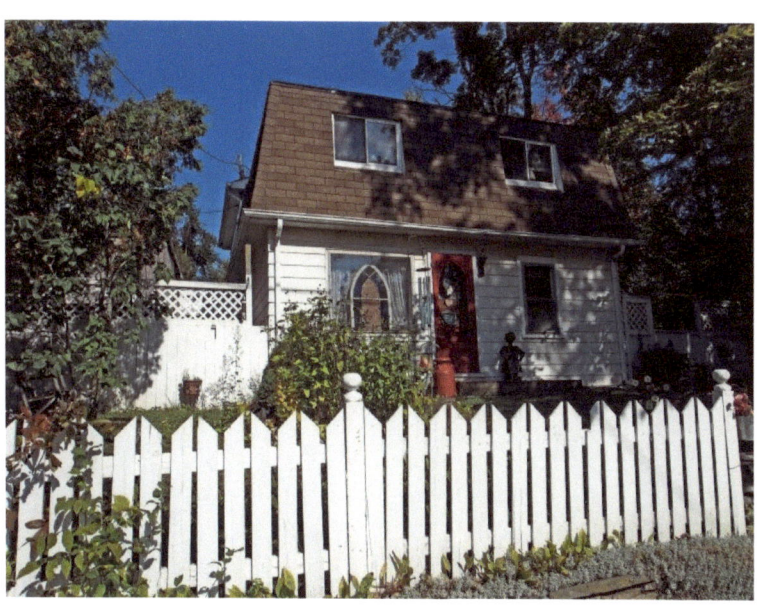

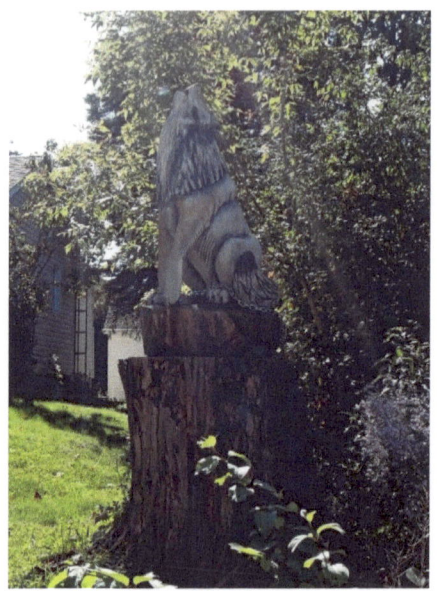

Howling wolf

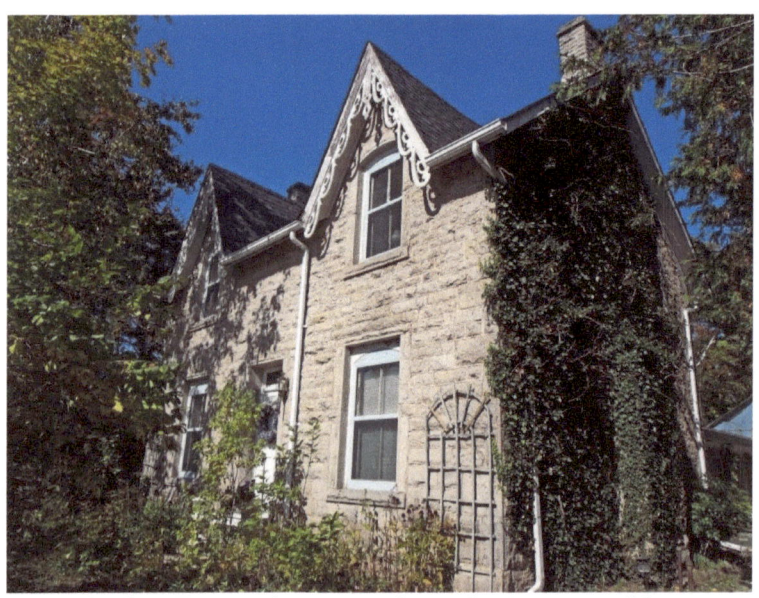

Gothic Revival – verge board trim on gables

Architectural Terms

Buttress: a masonry structure built against or projecting from a wall which serves to support or reinforce the wall. In Canadian architecture, they are sometimes used for decoration. Example: Limehouse Memorial Hall	
Cobblestone architecture: Refers to the use of cobblestones embedded in mortar as a method for erecting walls on houses and commercial buildings. Example: 149 Main Street, Rockwood	
Dentil Moulding: an even series of rectangles used as ornamental decoration in cornices. Example: 142 Main Street, Rockwood	
Dormer: (French for "sleep") a gable end window that pierces through the plane of a sloping roof surface to create usable space in the top floor or attic of a building by adding headroom. Example: 138 Alma Street, Rockwood	
Gable: the triangular portion of a wall between the edges of a sloping roof. Example: 225 Guelph Street, Rockwood	
Hipped Roof: a roof where all sides slope downwards to the walls with no gables. Example: 231 Guelph Street, Rockwood	
Iron Cresting: A decorative ornament along the top of a roof. Iron cresting was popular in the Baroque era and also in Italianate, Victorian, Second Empire and Queen Anne styles of architecture. Example: 130 Guelph Street	

Lancet Window: a tall, narrow window with a pointed arch at its top. Example: Limehouse Memorial Hall	
Pediment: a triangular section above the horizontal structure (entablature), typically supported by columns. The inside of the triangle is called the tympanum. Example: 477 Main Street, Rockwood Academy	
Portico: A covered porch area adjacent to a main entrance. The portico functions as a means to protect visitors from the elements as well as emphasizing the taste and wealth of the owner. Example: Rockwood Academy	
Quoin: masonry blocks at the corner of a wall, often a decorative feature, usually larger or of a different colour than the rest of the wall. Example: 130 Guelph Street, Rockwood	
Sidelight: a window, usually with a vertical emphasis, that flanks a door, and is often used to emphasize the importance of a primary entrance. Example: Rockwood Academy	
Transom Window: the light above the doorway, also called a fanlight. Example: Rockwood Academy	

Verge board and Finial: also called bargeboards – hang from the projecting end of a roof and are often elaborately carved and ornamented. **Finial:** ornament added to the top of a gable, pinnacle, canopy or spire – a Gothic element. Example: Limehouse	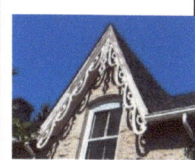
Voussoir: a wedge-shaped element used in building an arch. Example: 130 Guelph Street, Rockwood	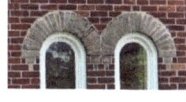

Georgian, before 1860 – This style began with the British King Georges in the 18th century. These buildings have balanced facades around a central door, medium-pitched gable roofs, and small paned windows. Example: Rockwood Academy	
Gothic Revival, 1830-1890 – These decorative buildings have sharply-pitched gables with highly detailed verge boards, pointed-arch window openings, and dichromatic brickwork. It is a common style in Ontario. Example: Main Street, Rockwood	
Italianate, 1850-1900 – It has wide-bracketed eaves, belvederes, wrap-around verandahs. Example: 231 Guelph Street, Rockwood	

A log cabin, built from logs, was usually one- or 1½-storeys constructed with round rather than hewn, or hand-worked, logs, and erected quickly for frontier shelter. Log cabins were built from logs laid horizontally and interlocked on the ends with notches. The pioneers chose old-growth trees that were straight and had few knots and did not need to be hewn to fit well together. Careful notching minimized the size of the gap between the logs and reduced the amount of chinking with sticks and rocks or daubing with mud to fill the gap. The length of one log was the length of one wall. Example: 145 Guelph Street, Rockwood	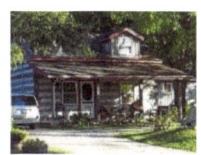
Romanesque Revival, 1880-1910 – This style hearkens back to medieval architecture of the 11th and 12th centuries with a heavy appearance, blocky towers and rounded arches. Example: 142 Main Street, Rockwood	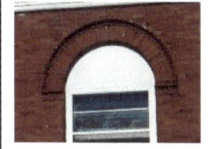

www.ingramcontent.com/pod-product-compliance
Lightning Source LLC
Chambersburg PA
CBHW040929180526
45159CB00002BA/669